Body Actions

Shelley Rotner and
David A. White

Holiday House / New York

The publisher would like to thank
pediatrician Dr. Kristin D'Aco for checking
the art and text of this book for accuracy.

Text and photographs copyright © 2012 by Shelley Rotner
Illustrations copyright © 2012 by Shelley Rotner and David A. White
All Rights Reserved
HOLIDAY HOUSE is registered in the U.S. Patent and Trademark Office.
Printed and Bound in May 2012 at Kwong Fat Offset Printing Co., Ltd.,
Dongguan City, China.
The text typeface is ITC Galliard.
www.holidayhouse.com
First Edition
1 3 5 7 9 10 8 6 4 2

Library of Congress Cataloging-in-Publication Data
Rotner, Shelley.
Body actions / Shelley Rotner and David A. White. — 1st ed.
p. cm.
ISBN 978-0-8234-2366-8 (hardcover)
1. Human body—Juvenile literature.
I. White, David A. (David Alan), 1973- ill.
II. Title.
QM27.R6759 2012
612—dc22
2011007268

Shelley and David dedicate the book to each other for their creative collaboration.

Every day you do so many things. How does your body do them?

How do you kick a ball, jump rope, blow up a balloon,

digest food, read a book, or ride a bike?

The human body is like an amazing machine
with many parts that work together.

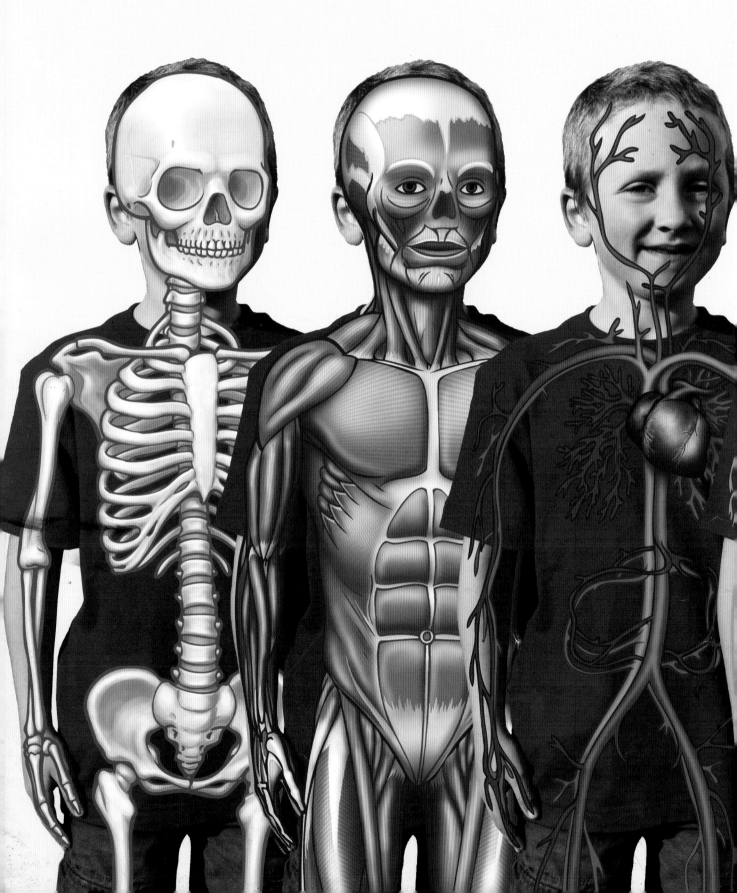

Each part has a special job to do.

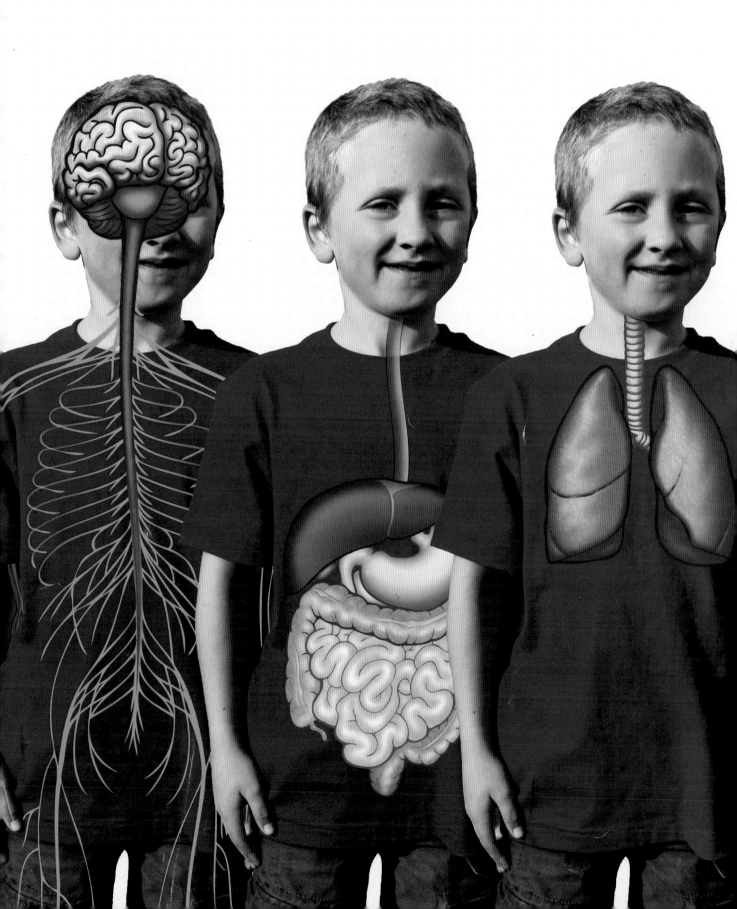

Your bones protect and support your body.

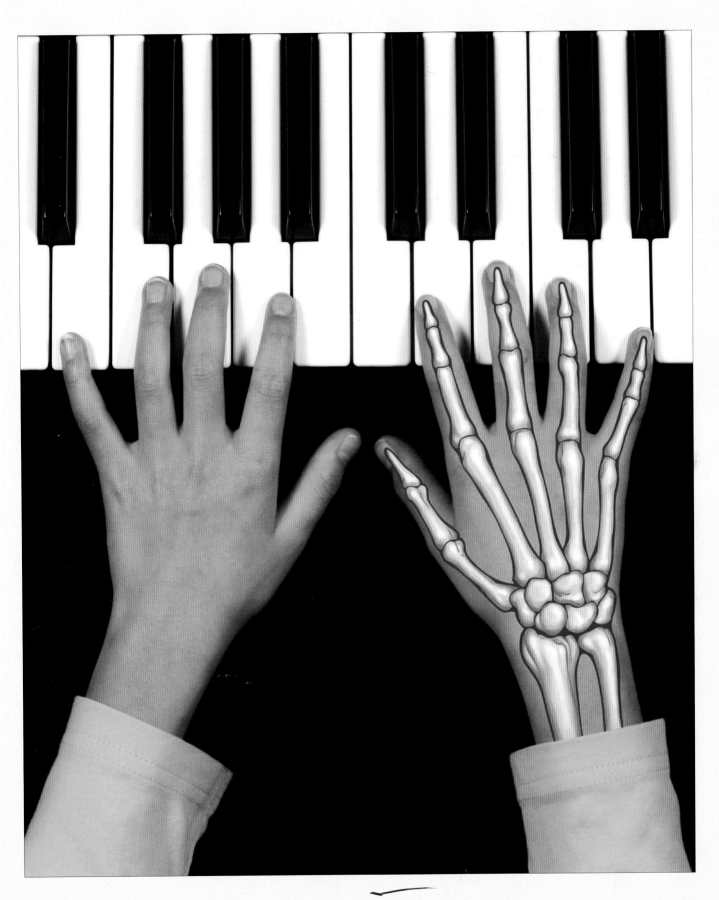

You have 206 bones in your body,
and more than 50 are in your hands.

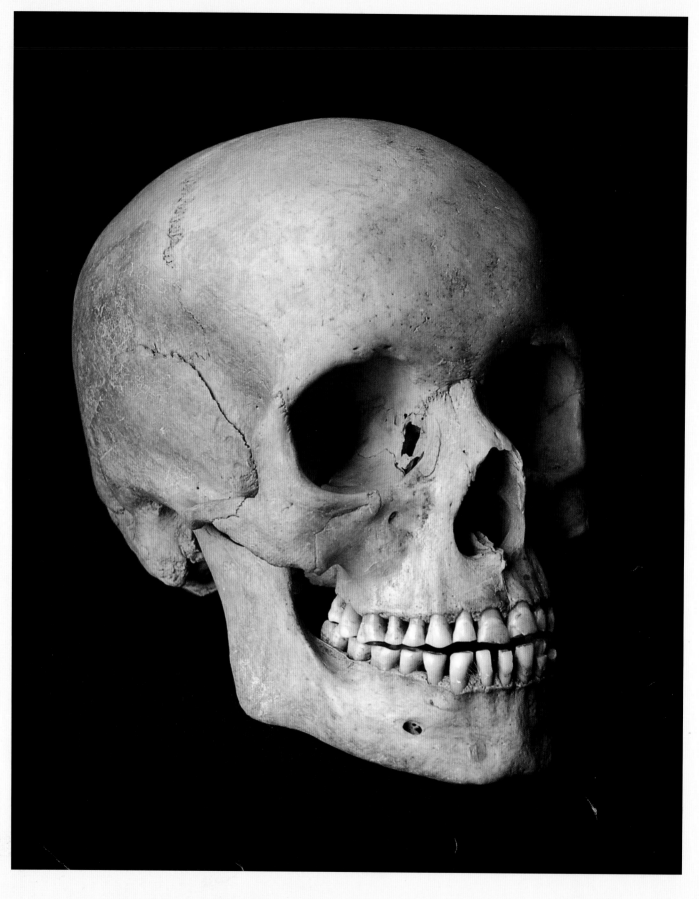

Your skull is made up of 22 bones that protect your brain and fit together like the pieces of a puzzle.

Your teeth are bones too.

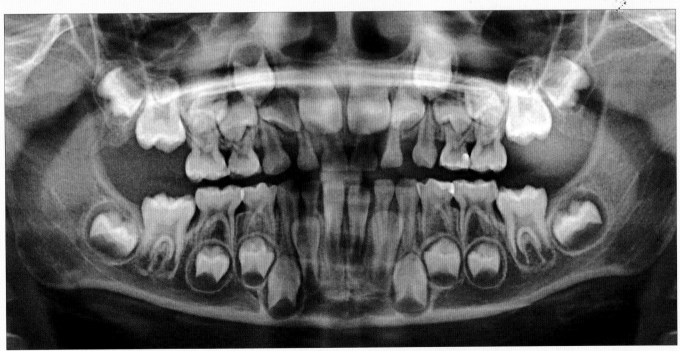

Children have 20 baby teeth that fall out and are replaced by 32 permanent teeth.

Muscles are the body's motors. They help you to move.

The muscles in your face help you blink,
eat, speak, smile, and frown.

You have about 650 muscles in your body.

Your heart is a muscle too.
It pumps blood to every part of your body,
delivering nourishment and oxygen.

Your heart is about the size of your fist and
beats about 70 to 80 times a minute—more than
100,000 times a day without resting.

The harder you work, the faster your heart beats.

You breathe air into and out of your lungs. With each breath, your lungs add fresh oxygen to your blood.

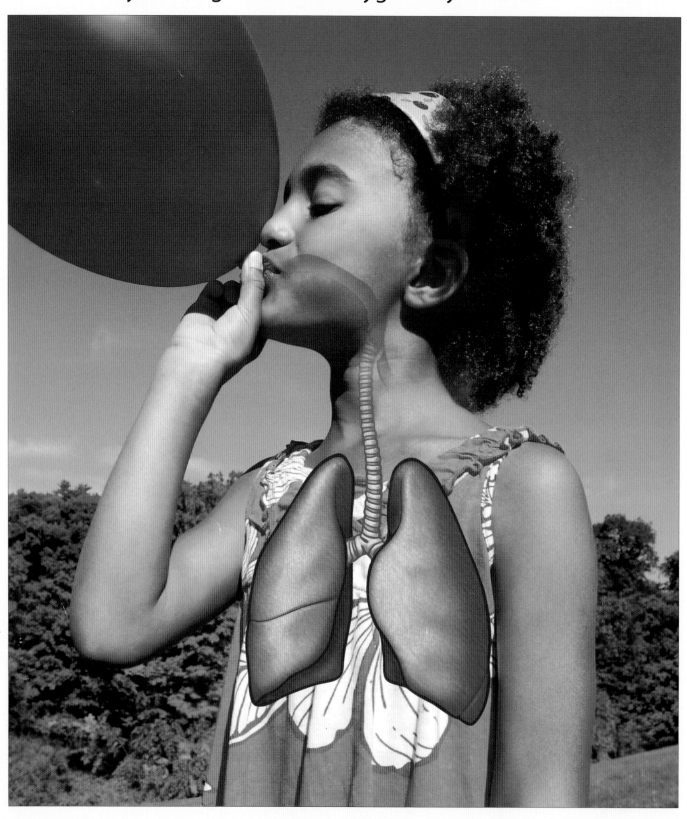

You take about 14 breaths a minute,
20,000 breaths a day, and more than 500 million in 70 years.

Digestion uses the food you eat as fuel
so that your body has the energy to work.

Your digestive tract is about six times longer
than you are tall if it was unfolded.
If you are 4 feet tall, your digestive tract is 24 feet long.

Your brain controls everything you do
by sending messages through your nerves.

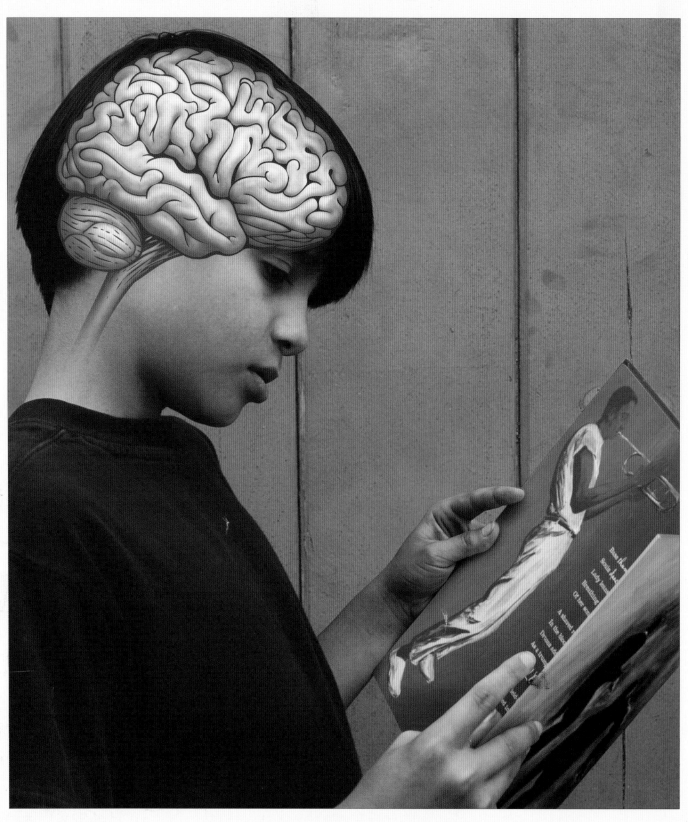

Nerves link your brain to every part of your body
so you can move, learn, feel, and grow.

Your brain never stops working, even when you're sleeping.

Your eyes are one of the most delicate and
complex parts of your body.

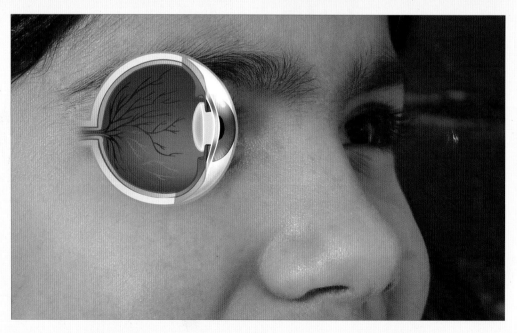

Each eye has a lens like a camera's
that lets in light so you can see.
You blink about fifteen times a minute.

You smell as you breathe air into your nose.

No two people smell something the same way.

Your ears work like funnels, allowing sounds to enter.
The sounds travel as waves of air.

The smallest bone in your body is inside your ear.

Your tongue is one of the strongest muscles in your body.
You have thousands of taste buds on your tongue.

 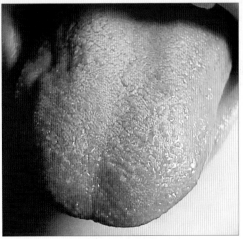

Taste buds tell you if food tastes salty, sour, sweet, or bitter.

Nerves in your skin tell you how something feels.
They tell you if something is hot, cold, smooth, rough, hard, or soft.

No two people have the same fingerprint.

Your skin is a waterproof shield that covers your body
and protects you from heat, cold, and germs.

Every day, small pieces of dead skin fall off.

Hair grows in many colors and textures on every part of your skin except on your lips, the palms of your hands, and the soles of your feet.

A hair lives for about 4 years and then falls out and is replaced by a new one.

Hair grows about 1/2 inch every month.

You need to eat well; keep your teeth, skin, and hair clean; and exercise regularly in order to stay healthy. You also need sleep so your body can rest.

You sleep about one-third of your life.

The 5 Senses

Sight—Your eyes gather visual information that your brain interprets. This allows you to see.

Smell—Scent enters your nose and comes into contact with the nerves that connect to your brain. This lets you smell.

Hearing—Your ears gather sound waves that travel down the tunnels to your eardrum. Nerves deep inside your ears bring this information to your brain so you hear.

Taste—Thousands of bumps called taste buds are on your tongue and the roof of your mouth. They are connected to nerves that carry this information to your brain so that you can taste.

Touch—Nerves throughout your body deliver information to your brain.

Skin and Hair

Skin is your largest organ and covers your entire body perfectly. It helps regulate your temperature. When you're hot, tiny pores open and let out sweat. When you're cold, you get goose bumps that make your hair stand up to keep you warm.

Hair not only helps regulate body temperature, but also protects your organs. Eyebrows and eyelashes help keep particles out of your eyes. Nose and ear hairs trap dust particles as they enter your body.

Body Systems

The different jobs your body does are classified into these systems:

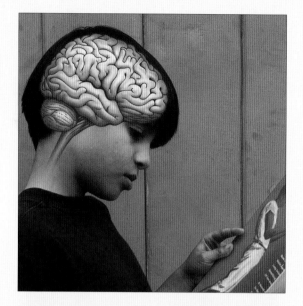

Your **Nervous System** is made up of your brain, your spinal cord, and all your nerves. It controls everything your body does. The spinal cord is an extension of your brain made up of nerves that connect to every part of your body.

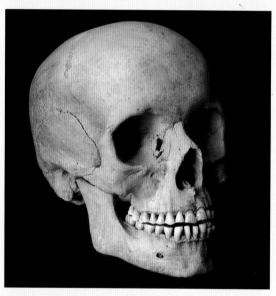

Your **Skeletal System** is the framework of bones that gives your body its shape. It also protects all the soft and sensitive parts inside your body and helps you move.

Your **Muscular System** controls the muscles in your body so that you can move. Your muscles move your joints much like a puppeteer makes the strings on a marionette move its parts.

Your **Respiratory System** brings fresh air into your two lungs and sends used air out with each breath. Your lungs are in your chest cavity. You can feel your chest rising and falling with your hand.

Your **Circulatory System** includes your heart, arteries, and veins. All together, they move blood throughout the body like a highway system. Your arteries deliver oxygen and nourishment from your heart. Your veins take blood back to your heart to get more oxygen and nourishment.

Your **Digestive System** breaks down, or digests, food so that your body can convert it into energy. The process starts with chewing and swallowing. In your stomach, food breaks down even more. After 2 to 6 hours, food passes into the long, folded tubes of your intestines. There, nourishment can be absorbed. Everything that isn't absorbed is passed out of your body.

Glossary

Arteries—are vessels that carry blood from the heart through the body.

Blood—is the liquid that circulates throughout your body delivering oxygen and food to your cells and taking away carbon dioxide and waste material.

Bones—are a rigid framework made mostly from minerals that make up the skeleton.

Brain—is an organ made up of billions of nerve cells that acts as headquarters for your body.

Cells—are called the building blocks of the body and are the smallest units of life. All living things are made up of cells. Cells are so tiny you can only see them under a microscope.

Intestines—the small and large intestines are tubes that help move food through the body, assisting in breaking down food so that it can be absorbed.

Joints—are where the bones in your body come together to meet other bones, allowing you to move in different directions.

Lungs—are a pair of organs inside your rib cage that take in oxygen so that it can be carried in the blood to cells.

Muscles—are fibers that tighten and relax to move parts of the body.

Nerves—are receptors and messengers. They receive and send information so that your body can perform and function.

Organs—are groups of different tissues working together to do special jobs. The heart, lungs, and stomach are all organs.

Rib cage—is made up of 12 pairs of curved rib bones that form a cage that protects the heart, lungs, and other organs.

Spinal cord—is made up of the nerves that travel from your brain down your back and connect to every part of your body, sending and receiving messages.

Veins—are vessels that carry blood deficient in oxygen back to the heart to get replenished.